People of the Ancient World

THE ANCIENT AZTECS

WRITTEN BY
LIZ SONNEBORN

Franklin Watts
A Division of Scholastic Inc.
New York Toronto London Auckland Sydney
Mexico City New Delhi Hong Kong
Danbury, Connecticut

Note to readers: Definitions for words in **bold** can be found in the Glossary at the back of this book.

Photographs © 2005: AP/Wide World Photos/Marco Ugarte: 96 bottom, 100 center; Art Resource, NY: 80, 81, 96 top left (Snark), 23 (John Bigelow Taylor), 9, 50, 51, 62, 94 (Werner Forman), 5, 12, 85, 97 top left (Michel Zabe); Bridgeman Art Library International Ltd., London/New York: 6 (Banco Mexicano de Imagenes/INAH), 55 (Biblioteca Medicea-Laurenziana, Florence, Italy), 41 (Jean-Pierre Courau), 100 bottom (Index); Corbis Images: 65 (Bettmann), 75 (Historical Picture Archive), 98 (Hulton-Deutsch), 67 (Douglas Peebles), 77 (Reuters); Mary Evans Picture Library: 100 top; Network Aspen/David Hiser: 4, 11, 13, 79, 97 top right; North Wind Picture Archives: 53, 96, 96 top right, 99; PhotoEdit/Gary Conner: 93, 97 bottom; Stone/Getty Images/David Hiser: 46; The Art Archive/Picture Desk: 27, 29, 43 (Bodleian Library Oxford/The Bodleian Library), 40 (Dagli Orti), 25, 61, 82 (Dagli Orti/Biblioteca Nacional Madrid), 8, 18, 70, 71, 95 (Dagli Orti/Museo Ciudad Mexico), 101 (Dagli Orti/Palazzo Pitti Florence), 21 (Natior Vautier), 33, 35, 59 (Mireille Vautier), 87 (Mireille Vautier/Antochiw Collection Mexico), 19 (Mireille Vautier/National Archives Mexico), 16, 37, 48, 90.

Cover art by Paine Profitt
Map by XNR Productions Inc.

Library of Congress Cataloging-in-Publication Data

Sonneborn, Liz.
  The ancient Aztecs / Liz Sonneborn.
  p. cm. — (People of the ancient world)
Includes bibliographical references and index.
ISBN 0-531-12362-6 (lib. bdg.) 0-531-16844-1 (pbk.)
1. Aztecs—History. 2. Aztecs—Social life and customs. I. Title. II. Series.
F1219.73.S66 2005
972.018—dc22
2004013909

Contents

"I WILL MAKE YOU LORDS AND KINGS of all that is in the world." According to myth, the god **Huitzilopochtli** predicted this glorious future for the ancient Aztec people. The ancestors of the Aztecs, known as the Mexica, were once a small band of people who eked out a meager existence in what is now northwest Mexico. But true to Huitzilopochtli's prophecy, by the fifteenth century, the Aztecs emerged as a powerful people that ruled over nearly all of **Mesoamerica**, an area including present-day Mexico, Guatemala, and Belize, and portions of Honduras and El Salvador. Between 1427 and 1521, the Aztecs controlled the greatest **empire** in what is now North America.

People of the Prickly Pear Cactus

The Mexica's original homeland was an island called Aztlán. It inspired the name "Aztec," which the Mexica would later adopt. In the thirteenth century, many Indian peoples from the region around Aztlán began moving south. Years of low rainfall had probably turned their surroundings into a sterile wilderness, forcing them to search out more fertile lands. These peoples eventually resettled in the Valley of Mexico, a lush area in what is now central Mexico. The Mexica was the last Indian group to head south.

Many Aztec myths tell the story of the Mexica's long and difficult journey. According to these stories, they traveled from place to place for many years. In some locations, they built houses and planted crops. But whenever they became comfortable in a new setting, Huitzilopochtli insisted they pick up and move again. Often, he made them leave before their crops were ready to be harvested, causing the Mexica to go hungry.

Finally, the Mexica arrived in the Valley of Mexico. This fertile region was already populated by other peoples, who feared the Mexica and drove them from every place they tried to settle. Desperate for a home, the Mexica begged the leader of the Culhua people for a land of their own. The leader agreed to let them settle in a barren area nearby that was full of lizards and snakes. With no food, the Mexica ate these animals to survive. In time, they prospered in the wilderness and earned the Culhua's respect. Living peacefully side by side, the Mexica and the Culhua people began marrying one another.

Huitzilopochtli was unhappy. He did not want the Mexica to live among the Culhua. He wanted the Mexica to be an independent people, living in a realm of their own. To turn the Culhua against the Mexica, Huitzilopochtli hatched a plan. He announced

According to legend, Huitzilopochtli made the Mexica relocate several times.

through his priests that he wanted to marry the daughter of the Culhua's leader. When the leader agreed, the Mexica brought the daughter to a temple and, on Huitzilopochtli's orders, killed her. The Mexica then dressed a young man in her skin and invited the Culhua leader to the temple for a ceremony in his daughter's honor. The leader happily joined in the ceremony until burning incense lit up the dark temple. When he saw the youth wearing his daughter's skin, he screamed and vowed to the destroy the Mexica.

Just as Huitzilopochtli had hoped, the Mexica fled from the Culhua's lands. Homeless again, they escaped into nearby marshlands. There, the Mexica searched for a sign promised by Huitzilopochtli. At last, they came upon an eagle eating a snake while perched on a great cactus. The cactus marked the sacred spot where Huitzilopochtli told them to build a city in his honor. On an island in Lake Texcoco, the Mexica's long migration ended, and their transformation into the Aztecs began.

Creating an Empire

When the Mexica arrived at Lake Texcoco, they were still a small group of people. But their many shared hardships had made them strong and determined. Against seemingly insurmountable odds, they set about fulfilling Huitzilopochtli's prophecy that they would become the kings of the world. They started building an enormous city called Tenochtitlán, meaning "place of the prickly pear cactus." At its center was a grand temple dedicated to Huitzilopochtli.

As they constructed Tenochtitlán, the Aztecs were inspired by tales of great peoples of the past. They particularly revered the Toltecs, who Aztec rulers later regarded as ancestors. Like the Aztecs, the Toltecs had come to the Valley of Mexico from the

The Mexica chose to settle at this site of Tenochtitlán when they saw an eagle perched on a cactus—a sign from the god Huitzilopochtli.

north. From about 900 to 1150, they used their military might to create a powerful empire. The Aztecs greatly admired the art and thought of the Toltecs. They explored the ruins of Tula, the Toltec capital, unearthing ancient sculptures, which Aztec artists faithfully copied.

Teotihuacán

Long before the Aztecs arrived in the Valley of Mexico, ancient Indians constructed a huge city in the region. At its height in the year 600, this great urban center had a population of between 125,000 and 200,000 people. The city was in ruins when the Aztecs first saw it. But what was left of the city's enormous buildings impressed them. They gave it the name Teotihuacán, meaning "Place of the Gods," and borrowed its layout for their own capital, Tenochtitlán.

The Aztecs also embraced the Toltecs' passion for war. In 1375, Acamapichtli became the first **tlatoani,** or supreme ruler of the Aztecs. During the reigns of the first three *tlatoque* (the plural of tlatoani), the Aztecs entered into battles as allies of their more powerful neighbors, the Tepaneca. But with the campaigns of the fourth tlatoani, Itzcoatl, the Aztecs emerged as the one great power in the region. The later tlatoque, especially Motecuhzoma I (also known as Montezuma) and Ahuitzotl, further expanded the empire. The growth of Tenochtitlán and other Aztec cities made **conquest** a necessity. Only by taking control of the wealth and land of peoples in outlying areas could the tlatoque support the Aztecs' increasing urban population. The leaders of conquered peoples often retained some power locally, but they could easily lose their positions if they displeased the tlatoani in Tenochtitlán.

In 1502, Motecuhzoma II became the ninth tlatoani. He was a skilled military leader, but by the time of his reign, there were few Mesoamerican peoples left for the Aztecs to conquer. In 1519, however, a new enemy arrived in their realm. A group of Spanish soldiers led by Hernán Cortés came to present-day Mexico in search of gold and other riches. The Spanish were awed by the Aztec Empire, particularly with the city of Tenochtitlán. Bernal Díaz del Castillo, a lieutenant of Cortés's, later wrote, "These great towns and pyramids and buildings rising from the water, all made of stone, seemed like an enchanted vision. . . . Indeed, some of our soldiers asked whether it was not all a dream."

Unfortunately for the Aztecs, the Spaniards' admiration for Tenochtitlán only excited their thirst for conquest. Cortés and his men first solicited the help of several Indian groups that resented the tlatoani's control over them. Together, the combined Spanish and Indian force attacked the Aztec capital in 1521. They burned the city, demolished temples, and smashed statues. Many other Aztec sites were destroyed or abandoned. Within a few years of their arrival, the Spanish invaders left the great Aztec Empire in ruins.

Learning About the Aztecs

Despite their rapid defeat by the Spanish and their allies, the Aztecs left behind an enormous amount of information about how they lived and what they thought. In fact, more is known about the Aztecs than about any other Indian people encountered by Europeans in the sixteenth century.

As with other ancient civilizations, **archaeology** provides modern scholars with many clues about Aztec culture. **Archaeologists** study the objects made and used by early peoples. These objects include portions of buildings, tools, pottery, and sculpture.

An archaeologist examines a sculpture found at Templo Mayor, an Aztec structure located in Mexico City, Mexico.

For centuries, the archaeological remains of the Aztecs were largely ignored. People constructed new settlements over the ruins of Aztec sites. For instance, Mexico City, now the capital of Mexico, was built over what was left of Tenochtitlán. While building these new settlements, people came upon Aztec objects buried deep in the ground. Few of these precious items, however, were preserved or studied.

In 1790, however, a great discovery sparked new interest in Aztec archaeology. Laborers digging a canal in Mexico City unearthed several monuments, including the Stone of the Sun. Also called the Aztec Calendar Stone, this huge, circular, carved

Also known as the Aztec Calendar Stone, the Stone of the Sun was discovered in Mexico City in 1790. The Aztecs had two types of calendars.

Templo Mayor

In 1978, workers from a power company in Mexico City made an astounding discovery. Digging in a downtown street, they found a massive round stone, measuring 11 feet (3.4 meters) across. Carved on its face was an image of Coyolxauhqui, the menacing sister of the Aztec god Huitzilopochtli.

The find marked the beginning of one of the greatest archaeological digs in Mexican history. Funded by the Mexican government, an excavation of the area where the stone was found began in the late 1970s. The archaeological team has uncovered the ruins of the Templo Mayor. This great pyramid-shaped structure once towered high above Tenochtitlán. The Aztecs considered the temple to be the center of the universe. The ruins of the Templo Mayor are now open to the public. The site attracts millions of visitors each year.

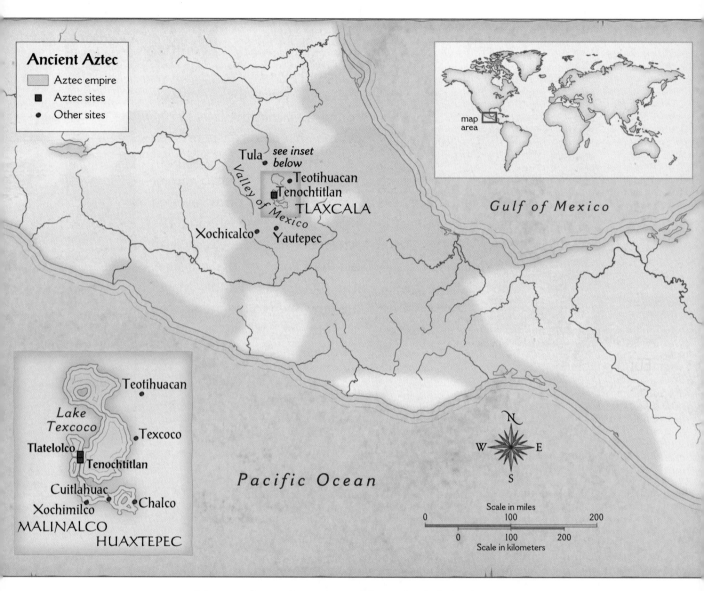

Ancient Aztec

- Aztec empire
- ■ Aztec sites
- • Other sites

Tula
see inset below
Teotihuacan
■ Tenochtitlan
TLAXCALA
Valley of Mexico
Xochicalco
Yautepec

Gulf of Mexico

map area

Inset:

Teotihuacan
Lake Texcoco
Texcoco
Tlatelolco
■ Tenochtitlan
Cuitlahuac
Chalco
Xochimilco
MALINALCO
HUAXTEPEC

Pacific Ocean

N
W   E
S

Scale in miles
0   100   200

0   100   200
Scale in kilometers

This map shows the traditional homeland of the Aztecs.

sculpture is perhaps the most famous of all surviving Aztec art-works. This find excited the people of Mexico, who were then still living under Spanish control. In the coming decades, Mexicans grew more curious about their Aztec ancestors as they began to seek independence from the Spanish. In 1821, Mexico finally became an independent nation. The new government established the Museo Nacional de Antropología (National Museum of Anthropology), where Aztec **artifacts** are now preserved as national treasures.

In recent years, archaeologists have studied many important Aztec sites in Mexico. Among the most notable is the **excavation** of the Templo Mayor, the great ceremonial center of Tenochtitlán. This archaeological research is helping to reshape much of what is known about how the Aztecs worshipped.

Archaeology provides the only means of studying some ancient cultures. But there are other important sources of information about the Aztecs. Among these sources are the writings of the Spanish. The defeat of the Aztecs fascinated the people of Europe. Several Spanish soldiers tried to satisfy the public's curiosity by writing accounts of the attack. Perhaps the most famous account was Bernal Díaz del Castillo's *True History of the Conquest of New Spain* (1632). Cortés himself wrote a series of letters to Charles I, the king of Spain, that gave detailed descriptions of his impressions of the Aztecs and their ways.

Soon after the Spanish conquest, priests from Spain arrived in present-day Mexico. Their mission was to convert the Indians to Christianity, but they also devoted themselves to studying Aztec culture. Based on extensive interviews with Aztec elders, they created enormous encyclopedias about Aztec customs and religious beliefs. Many of these books, called codices (the plural of **codex**), were illustrated with paintings made by Aztec artists.

The Aztecs also wrote their own books. Government officials kept detailed records about the peoples under their rule, and Aztec scholars used picture writing to compile histories, calendars, and almanacs. A few of these codices have survived in their

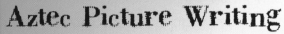

Aztec Picture Writing

Unlike many Indian peoples, the Aztecs developed a mode of writing. It made use of symbols known as glyphs. Glyphs could represent people, places, things, dates, or concepts. Picture writing was a collection of glyphs, which readers used to jog their memories about a story or an event. From generation to generation, glyphs aided Aztec storytellers in reciting tales of their people's history.

original forms. Others exist only in translations made by the Spanish. But they give today's scholars a perspective on the Aztecs not available to students of other ancient Indian peoples who did not keep written records. These records tell the Aztecs' own story of their days as a great and powerful people.

Chapter I

COMMONERS, NOBLES, AND RULERS

When the Aztecs first came to the Valley of Mexico, all the people lived in much the same way. All Aztecs worked the land, struggling to raise enough food to survive. But Aztec society changed as the empire grew and prospered. Work became more specialized. Some Aztecs continued to farm, but produced enough food to allow others to find different ways to make a living. People in these new professions included warriors, priests, administrators, merchants, and artisans. Over time, Aztec society also divided into two social classes, the **macehualtin** and the **pipiltin**.

The Common People

About nineteen Aztecs out of every twenty were macehualtin, or commoners. These people did most of the backbreaking work of building the empire, from farming its fields to constructing its great cities. They served in the military and imported goods from foreign peoples. They also made the beautiful jewelry, ornaments, and clothing worn by the pipiltin, the 5 percent of the population that belonged to the noble class.

Although grouped together as commoners, the status of individuals within the macehualtin varied enormously. Talented warriors, merchants, and craftspeople could become very wealthy. On the other hand, in times of **famine** or economic downturn, common laborers could become so poor that they had to sell themselves and their children into slavery.

The macehualtin spent their lives serving the pipiltin. But few commoners were angry about their inferior status. From birth,

Quetzalcoatl

All Aztec nobles traced their ancestry back to Quetzalcoatl, a fabled ruler of the Toltecs. In about 1150, the Toltec capital of Tula was destroyed. Ancient stories held that Quetzalcoatl abandoned the city, traveling east to the Gulf of Mexico. In one story, he then set himself on fire and became a star. In another, he sailed away on a raft made of snakes, vowing to return one day.

the Aztecs were taught to accept the social order. They learned that the gods themselves had given the pipiltin their elevated positions. Commoners who dared to behave like nobles were considered dangerous people. They risked unleashing harmful forces into the world that could contaminate their families and neighbors.

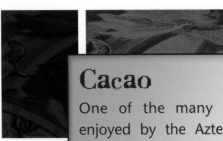

Cacao

One of the many privileges enjoyed by the Aztec nobility was the right to drink cacao, a bitter chocolate beverage made from the ground seeds of the cacao tree. Commoners were not allowed to drink cacao, but even if they had been, few could have afforded it. The cacao tree did not grow well in the Aztecs' territory, so the beans, imported from lands far to the south, were extremely expensive.

Life Among the Pipiltin

The term *pipiltin* literally means "children of someone important." As the translation suggests, nobles inherited their social status. Almost always, nobles retained their positions from birth to death. If a noble person committed a particularly terrible crime, however, he and his family could be made commoners as punishment.

Nobles were careful to keep their lineages free of macehualtin blood. A noble could only marry another noble. A noble man sometimes had more than one wife, because marriage was a common way of bonding important noble families to one another. Such bonds were also maintained through gift-giving. At ceremonies and social occasions, nobles often exchanged lavish presents, such as ornaments made from gold and precious stones. These gifts helped create or strengthen the ties between their families.

Laws helped nobles maintain their status. In the mid-fifteenth century, the tlatoani Motecuhzoma I issued a legal code that made an Aztec's social class clear to all. It declared that only nobles could wear cotton clothes. A commoner who defied the

tegal

Uamále tea pay tegal

la insignia

dias del fuego
Xuo tecutL

Els cavatL

Els ca vatL

A nobleman participates in an initiation ceremony.

law would be put to death. Other privileges legally granted to people of noble birth included the right to wear gold ornaments and to live in two-story houses.

Nobles led comfortable lives. They wore beautiful clothing and ate fresh meat, fish, and vegetables. Some lived in the grand palaces of the tlatoani or of the local leaders they served. Many nobles had huge estates with large staffs of commoners to keep house and tend fields.

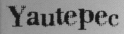
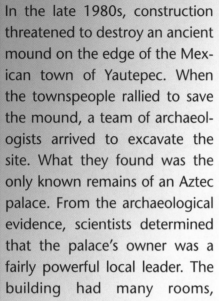

Yautepec

In the late 1980s, construction threatened to destroy an ancient mound on the edge of the Mexican town of Yautepec. When the townspeople rallied to save the mound, a team of archaeologists arrived to excavate the site. What they found was the only known remains of an Aztec palace. From the archaeological evidence, scientists determined that the palace's owner was a fairly powerful local leader. The building had many rooms, courtyards, and passageways. Its thick stone walls were covered with plaster painted with colorful murals.

Excavations of nearby areas suggest the palace lay next to a neighborhood of wealthy Aztecs. Even the houses of commoners at Yautepec indicate the area was prosperous. Among the artifacts discovered there were items made from costly imported materials, such as copper and bronze.

Burdens of the Noble Class

Being a noble, however, carried some responsibilities. Noble girls and boys learned about these at the **calmecac**, special schools attached to temples. These schools were designed to educate nobles, though if a commoner proved particularly promising or talented, he or she might be invited to attend one. Under the strict supervision of priests, calmecac students were taught to meditate and pray. As religious observances, they fasted, often for days. They also cut their legs, arms, and earlobes, offering their own blood as a sacrifice to their gods.

At the calmecac and at home, young nobles were constantly instructed in how to behave. Elders told them to work hard and to live humbly. Youths were cautioned not to overeat or wear excessively ornate clothing. They were also expected to learn about Aztec history and customs by studying books and paintings.

When they reached adulthood, noble men went to work for the empire. Some became priests. Others became warriors, joining the Eagle Knights or Jaguar Knights, two military orders made up entirely of nobles. Still others became judges. Judges settled disputes among the Aztecs and directed the work of police forces. They had the power to arrest anyone, even high officials. If a judge abused his authority by accepting a bribe, he often paid for his crime with his life.

Many nobles became administrators. The larger the Aztec Empire became, the more people were needed to oversee it. Noble administrators organized common workers to build roads, construct buildings, and cultivate land.

Another important duty of administrators was to help collect **tribute**. Tribute was similar to a tax levied on all Aztec citizens. No matter how they made their living, Aztecs were expected to provide some kind of goods or services to the tlatoani. For instance, farmers had to give up part of their harvest, while artisans offered handcrafted objects, such as bowls, jewelry, or elaborate uniforms for the empire's warriors.

Eagle Knights were a group of noble warriors.

Keeping track of who paid what tribute was a huge task that fell to clerks from the noble class. In addition, noble tax collectors traveled all over the empire, pressuring citizens to pay any overdue tribute. According to the Spanish writer Bernal Díaz del Castillo, tax collectors were privileged and powerful men. Díaz wrote, "They wore rich embroidered cloaks, loin-cloths of the same nature, and their shining hair was raised in a knot on their heads . . . . and other Indians, like servants, fanned them with fly-whisks." He noted that when a group of tax collectors arrived in one city, local rulers "went pale, and began to tremble with fear."

Ruling the Aztecs

The most feared person in the Aztec Empire, however, was the tlatoani. From the capital of Tenochtitlán, this ruler made decisions that affected all the Aztecs. The tlatoani was more than a political leader. He was also a military commander and a religious figure. In fact, once the tlatoani ascended to the throne, in the Aztecs' eyes, he became superhuman, making him worthy of his people's total submission.

A tlatoani held his position for life. When a tlatoani died, his successor was one of his male relatives who was chosen by a council of nobles. Usually, the successor was the former tlatoani's son or brother, but he could also be a nephew or grandson. In making its choice, the council considered which candidate showed the highest moral character and the greatest promise as a leader. An Aztec noble described for Spanish priest Bernardino de Sahagún the traits a tlatoani had to have: "The good ruler [is] a protector; one who carries [his subjects] in his arms, who unites them, who brings them together. He rules, takes responsibilities, assumes burdens. He carries [his subjects] in his cape; he bears them in his arms."

An illustration shows Motecuhzoma II becoming the Aztec ruler.

Before taking office, the new tlatoani was the focus of an elaborate coronation. Local leaders from all over the empire were expected to attend the ceremony. Even rulers of the Aztecs' enemies were invited. The coronation was a religious ceremony, but it also served a political purpose. Both allies and enemies were sure to leave the event impressed by the tlatoani's wealth and power.

On the first day of the coronation ritual, the new tlatoani was stripped naked and led to the top of a pyramid-shaped temple in the center of Tenochtitlán. He then spent four days hidden away, during which elders recited the *huehuetlatolli,* the "old, old speeches." In these lectures they warned the tlatoani of the awesome responsibility he was taking on. They also urged him to make his people content and to keep order within his realm: "Gladden, gather, unite, humor, please thy noblemen, thy rulers. And make the city happy. Arrange each [citizen] in his proper place."

When the tlatoani emerged from seclusion, he hosted a great feast and received luxurious gifts from his many guests. Wearing a gold crown while sitting atop a throne decorated with eagle feathers and jaguar hides, the tlatoani's transformation was complete. As one elder told a tlatoani during his coronation, "You are no longer a human being like us; we no longer see you as merely human."

The tlatoani settled into a life of extraordinary luxury. Bernal Díaz del Castillo left a detailed record of the palace of Motecuhzoma II, where the tlatoani was attended by more than six hundred nobles. The palace was more elegant than any the Spaniard had ever seen. Stretching across 6 acres (2.4 hectares), it included quarters for high-ranking warriors, judges, priests, and artisans as well as lush gardens, an aviary, and a zoo. Nightly, the tlatoani presided over a lavish feast at which as many as three hundred dishes were served. While he dined on delicacies from

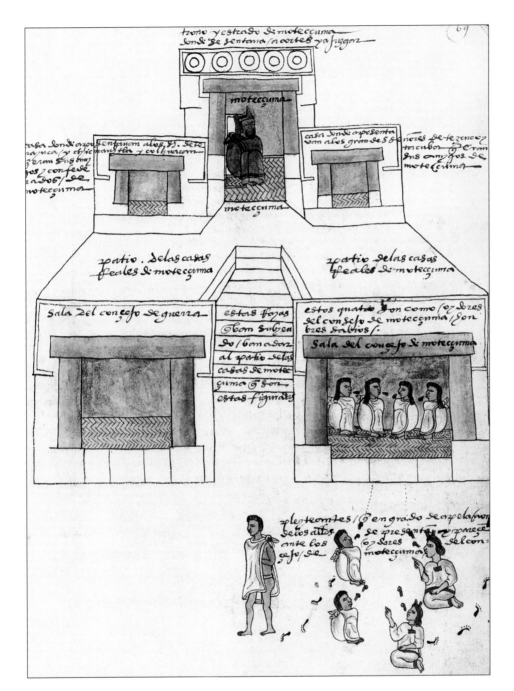

This drawing shows Motecuhzoma II in the upper chamber of his palace while his advisers meet below.

every part of the empire, singers, dancers, and jesters entertained his entourage. With his lifestyle financed by his subjects' tribute, the tlatoani could afford to live a privileged life befitting his godlike status.

Chapter II

WARRIORS

According to myth, Huitzilopochtli, the great god who led the Aztecs to their homeland, was the son of Coatlicue. She was impregnated with him by a ball of feathers that fell from the sky. When Coatlicue became pregnant, her daughter Coyolxauhqui was convinced that her mother had shamed the family. Coyolxauhqui and her four hundred brothers decided to murder Coatlicue and her unborn child. But before they could act, Huitzilopochtli burst from Coatlicue's womb and killed his plotting siblings. The slain Coyolxauhqui became the moon, and her dead brothers became the stars.

The story of Huitzilopochtli's birth was important to the Aztecs. It established that their most important god was a warrior. It also encouraged them to fight their enemies just as ferociously as Huitzilopochtli had fought Coyolxauhqui.

The Culture of War

Skilled warriors were among the most revered people in Aztec society. They were honored according to a highly organized ranking system. With each battlefield success, warriors rose in rank and earned the right to wear increasingly elaborate battle gear. For instance, after taking his first war captive, a warrior received a cloak decorated with flowers. After taking four

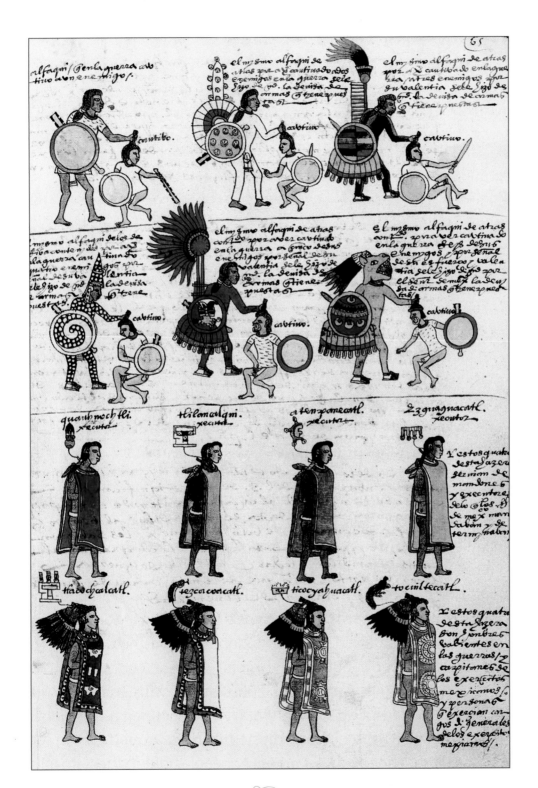

The six stages
of a successful
priest-warrior
appear in the top
two rows. Below
several types of
imperial officers
are shown.

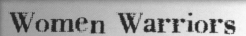

Women Warriors

Generally, Aztec women did not engage in warfare. But during childbirth, women were considered warriors. As they went through labor, midwives let out war cries, rallying them to a successful delivery. In the Aztecs' eyes, women won a battle when they gave birth to a child, who they likened to a captive taken in war. Like warriors slain on the battlefield, women who died in childbirth became the sun's companions in the afterlife.

captives, a fighter was honored with a jaguarskin uniform, worn so his head emerged from the dead animal's mouth. Special military societies were open only to those who had taken many war captives and had performed at least twenty acts of bravery in battle. Most of the highest-ranking warriors were nobles, but the Aztecs also honored commoners with great military exploits to their credit.

Training for war started early. In school, Aztec boys were put through military drills. They learned to handle the Aztecs' favorite battle weapon, a wooden club studded with sharp bits of **obsidian** (volcanic glass). Experienced warriors also told students war stories and showed them the beautiful uniforms they could one day wear. Boys began their military careers by carrying a warrior's supplies to the battlefield. Families fought to have their sons serve under the most distinguished warriors.

Whenever the tlatoani, in consultation with a council of nobles, decided to go to war, the Aztecs assembled a new fighting force. The tlatoani was expected to have a good reason for any attack planned against a weaker people. Often, the tlatoani's enemies gave him all the justification he needed. For instance, if traveling Aztec merchants were killed in a foreign territory, the tlatoani had ample excuse to declare war. But if the tlatoani was eager to fight a particularly hated enemy, he would use the slightest motive to justify raising an army. In one example, the tlatoani Axayacatl wanted to bring the town of Tlatelolco into the Aztec Empire. He used insults hurled at Aztec women in the town marketplace to justify launching a military campaign.

Before the fighting began, the tlatoani sent out ambassadors to meet with the enemy leader. Along with gifts, they offered the leader a chance to avoid war by agreeing to join the empire. If he did, he would usually be allowed to retain his position as a local leader. In some cases, he could even avoid having to pay tribute to the tlatoani.

If the enemy leader refused, the ambassadors returned to Tenochtitlán, and the war preparations began. An army was assembled, and the tlatoani started collecting food and other supplies for the warriors from his stores of tribute goods. For a major, long-distance campaign, the tlatoani would have to gather provisions for as many as 200,000 men.

As part of his war preparations, the tlatoani also sent out spies to scout the enemy's territory. Spying could be dangerous. If a spy was caught by the enemy, he would be executed. Based on the spies' reports, the tlatoani drew up the battle plans. At the same time, priest-warriors set out for the battlefield. There, they called on supernatural forces to aid the Aztec army in the fight to come.

On the Battlefield

In the Aztec war strategy there was no element of surprise. The ambassadors announced to the enemy the place and day they would meet the Aztec army. Aztec warriors instead relied on their superior training and discipline. When they reached the battlefield, they lined up in battle formation according to the orders of their military leaders. The officers severely punished any soldier who disobeyed orders. According to Spanish priest Bernardino de Sahagún, "No one might break ranks or crowd in among the others; they would then and there slay or beat whoever would bring confusion or crowd in among the others."

The priest-warriors blew into conch shells to signal the start of the battle. As the Aztec warriors rushed forward, they filled the air with war cries. As one Spaniard wrote, "During combat they sing and dance and sometimes give the wildest shouts and whistles imaginable, especially when they know they have the advantage. Anyone facing them for the first time can be terrified by their screams and their ferocity."

The Aztecs fought enemy soldiers fiercely but did not try to destroy their towns. The tlatoani wanted to conquer the settlements intact so that their residents would be able to start paying tribute as soon as possible. There was one exception, however. Aztec fighters did everything they could to burn down the temple in the enemy's town. In the Aztecs' rules of battle, the burning of the temple immediately marked the end of the battle and the defeat of the enemy. Symbolically, the temple's destruction told the enemy they were no longer free to worship their local gods. Instead, they had become Aztec citizens who would have to recognize Huitzilopochtli as their ruling deity.

As soon as the Aztecs declared victory, the defeated leaders began negotiating what kind and how much tribute they would be required to pay the tlatoani. Meanwhile, messengers ran back to Tenochtitlán to report on the battle. The tlatoani wanted to know how many warriors had been killed and which of the survivors had distinguished themselves in battle.

A mural depicts the Aztecs fighting the Tlaxcaltecs, one of the other peoples in the region.

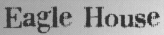

Eagle House

In the late 1970s, archaeologists began excavating the main ceremonial complex of the Aztec capital of Tenochtitlán. Among their finds was Eagle House. The structure was the meeting place of the Eagle Knights, an important military order open only to nobles.

Inside Eagle House were beautiful statues and carvings celebrating the culture of war. On each side of a doorway were two life-size sculptures of Eagle warriors. Originally, the figures were painted and held real weapons in their hands. Along the wall of a patio in Eagle House was a low bench carved with a procession of warriors. The carvings imitated the art style of the Toltecs, an ancient people the Aztecs admired for their military exploits.

Taking Captives

When the warriors returned, ceremonies were held to celebrate the victory. Before the crowds, the tlatoani praised the widows of fallen warriors for their sacrifice. He reminded them that their husbands would be well rewarded for dying on the battlefield. In the afterlife, they would rise into the sky and join the sun as it traveled across the sky each day. In a speech to grieving widows, one tlatoani explained that the dead warriors "have departed holding each other's hands. . . . [They] are now rejoicing in the shining place of the sun, where they walk about in his company, embellished with his light."

The tlatoani rewarded the bravest warriors with gifts, such as colorful capes and ornaments. Particularly honored were those who had captured enemy fighters, because taking captives was

Through warfare, the Aztecs sought to capture their enemies. These prisoners were sometimes sacrificed to the gods.

one of the primary goals of warfare. In fact, Aztec warriors achieved much more prestige from taking an opponent captive than from killing one.

The Aztecs needed war captives to sacrifice to the gods. Human sacrifice played a central role in the Aztec view of the world. The Aztecs believed that the universe was fragile. At any moment, supernatural forces could become unbalanced, sending the world into chaos. The only way to keep the universe in balance

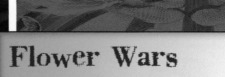

Flower Wars

In times of peace, the Aztecs faced a problem. They did not have enough war captives to satisfy their gods' demands for human sacrifice. To ensure that they had a steady supply of captives, the Aztecs invented *xochiyaoyotl*, meaning "flower wars." In xochiyaoyotl, two communities within the Aztec Empire agreed to battle one another. Warriors who took captives during xochiyaoyotl received the same honors bestowed in real wars against foreign enemies.

was to nourish the gods with offerings of human blood. According to Aztec myth, the gods made the first humans from their own blood. Human beings, therefore, owed a debt to the supernatural world that could be paid only by shedding blood themselves.

Most Aztecs at some point in their lives engaged in bloodletting. To ask the gods for help, they cut their flesh. Most often, they pierced their earlobes with cactus thorns, though sometimes they cut their legs, arms, or chests, pulling a reed through the hole. Priests engaged in bloodletting daily. Their ears were often permanently shredded by the ritual.

Heart Sacrifices

The greatest offering the Aztecs could make to the gods, however, was the heart of a living person. In the Aztecs' worldview, the victims of heart sacrifices gave their lives so the Aztecs could live. Accordingly, they were honored as the "divine dead." The

Aztecs called their hearts "eagle cactus-fruits" and their blood "precious water."

Heart sacrifices were performed during complex rituals performed high atop temples, where they could be seen by crowds of onlookers. Amid clouds of incense, priests lay the victim down on a sacrificial stone and held down his arms and legs. In one

A priest performs a heart sacrifice, which was the greatest offering the Aztecs could give their gods.

swift move, the priest cut into the victim's chest. According to a noble interviewed by Bernardino de Sahagún, the executioner "at once seized [the victim's] heart. And he whose breast he laid open was quite alive. And when [the priest] had seized his heart, he dedicated it to the sun." The victim's body was then rolled down the temple stairs, leaving a trail of blood.

Many ancient peoples practiced human sacrifice. But no other civilization performed sacrificial rituals on as large a scale as did the Aztecs. They performed as many as twenty thousand heart sacrifices a year.

The Spaniards who arrived in the Aztecs' lands in the early sixteenth century were soldiers familiar with the carnage of the battlefield. But even they were disturbed by the violence of human sacrifice. Spanish soldier Bernal Díaz del Castillo wrote of coming upon a temple where a sacrifice had recently taken place: "Here we found five Indians who had been sacrificed to them on that very night. Their chests had been struck open and their arms and thighs cut off, and the walls of these buildings were covered with blood. All this amazed us greatly."

Undoubtedly, this reaction was shared by many of the Aztecs who watched the bloody rituals. While they believed these ceremonies were necessary to keep the world in order, they surely also learned a lesson from what they saw. By orchestrating these rituals, the tlatoani reminded his people of his power. Anyone thinking of defying his rule was likely to think again after seeing the temple steps stained deep red with enemy blood.

Chapter III

PRIESTS AND SCHOLARS

"[T]hey lead us, they guide us, they tell us the way." Aztec nobles used these words in 1524 to explain the awesome responsibilities of the **tlamatinime,** or "wise men." Called priests by the Spanish, the tlamatinime were entrusted with keeping the Aztecs' religious traditions alive. It fell to them to teach the Aztecs about their gods and to lead them in worship. The priests were also responsible for performing certain religious rituals that kept the universe in balance. As keepers of this sacred knowledge, the tlamatinime held the very fate of the Aztec world in their hands.

The World of the Gods

The Aztecs' religious beliefs centered around the idea of *teotl*, or sacred energy. This force was concentrated in the gods they worshipped. When the Spanish insisted the Aztecs give up their gods, the Aztec priests tried to explain that they could not imagine existing without them: "[T]here is life because of the gods; with their sacrifice they gave us life. . . . [The gods] provide our subsistence, all that we eat and drink, that which maintains life."

The Aztecs recognized some two hundred gods. Each ruled over different aspects of the world, but their realms often overlapped. The myths told about the gods also frequently contradicted

The Stone of Tizoc

Discovered in the 1790s, the Stone of Tizoc is one of the best-known Aztec sculptures. On the edge of this large, circular stone, Aztec artisans carved a great sundisk. On its side was a procession of warriors led by the tlatoani Tizoc. The warriors are shown dragging the gods of conquered towns by their hair. Depicting these foreign gods as war captives, the carvings illustrate the Aztecs' willingness to take over other peoples' gods and add them their own list of deities.

each other. This was because the roster of gods was always changing. Many of the Aztec gods had their origins in earlier Indian cultures, but others were borrowed from the peoples they conquered.

The Aztecs' gods had certain characteristics. For instance, their most important water god, Tlaloc, wore a costume of rich turquoise

Opposite: A wall painting shows an Aztec priest praying. In the Aztec religion, there were approximately two hundred gods.

41

blue. Tlaltecuhtli, the main earth god, was depicted as a crouching monster, and Mictlantecuhtli, the god of the underworld, appeared as a ghoulish skeleton.

Some professions had special patron gods. Weavers, merchants, and goldsmiths, for instance, each had a god they called upon for protection. Neighborhoods often had their own gods to look after the residents' interests.

Worshipping the Gods

The Aztecs believed that by properly honoring the gods, they could ensure their own well-being. Every Aztec home had a shrine with simple wooden sculptures of gods. Aztecs asked these sculptures for help with everyday problems. For instance, a fisher might ask Chalchiuhtlicue, the goddess of lakes and rivers, to give him a good catch. The Aztecs also communicated with supernatural forces through small, daily rituals. Spanish priest Bernardino de Sahagún recorded that when women cooked corn, they always took a moment to soothe the plant's spiritual energy: "[F]irst of all they breathed upon [the corn]. . . . In this way it would not take fright; thus it would not fear the heat."

The primary responsibility for worshipping the gods fell to the priests. They received training in their priestly duties at the calmecac, the schools for noble youths. These trainees were called **tlamacazton** meaning "little priests." Most were young nobles, but commoners with exceptional talent were sometimes allowed to join the priesthood. Nearly all priests were men, but occasionally a woman served in the priesthood until she was ready to marry.

For a year, the tlamacazton underwent intensive instruction. They were taught to perform rituals and memorized prayers. During much of their training, they survived on little food, eating

A page from the
Codex Mendoza
shows religious
and military
training options
for boys.

God Impersonators

In some Aztec rituals, a god was impersonated by a human. For instance, for the feast of Tezcatlipoca, the god impersonator was chosen from the young male war captives. The impersonator had to be smart and physically attractive. For a full year before the ceremony, he was trained to act like Tezcatlipoca while he lived in luxury, attended by nobles and priests. On the feast day, the impersonator sang and played a flute as he approached the temple where he would be sacrificed.

only small meals twice a day. To purify their bodies, the tlamacazton took ritual baths.

Those who completed this rigorous training program became full priests, entitled to wear the long black cloaks and gowns of their office. Priests also dyed their faces and bodies black. They let their hair grow long, sometimes all the way down to their feet. It was matted down flat with blood from their ears, which they cut daily in bloodletting rituals to please the gods. Bernal Díaz del Castillo wrote that, because of their role in human sacrifices, "they stank like sulphur and they had another bad smell like carrion [decaying flesh]." But Díaz del Castillo also noted that the priests were highly respected as moral leaders: "[W]e heard it said that these priests were very pious and led good lives."

Duties of the Priesthood

Aztec priests had many duties and responsibilities, the most important of which was performing rituals. As the guardians of sacred knowledge, they organized and orchestrated a wide variety of ceremonies. They said the proper prayers, played music, burned incense, and made offerings to the gods. Human sacrifices were overseen by an **elite** group of priests known as the *tlenamacac*, or fire priests.

In addition to supervising the Aztecs' ceremonial life, priests were responsible for the management of the temples. Temples were built throughout the Aztec Empire. In fact, every Aztec god had at least one temple dedicated to his or her worship. Priests organized workers to construct these temples and then managed the staff needed to maintain them properly. Keeping temples in good order was painstaking work. They were full of sacred objects that had to be cleaned constantly to keep them pure. Among these objects were statues of the gods and sacred bundles made of feathers, stones, and other items of religious importance wrapped in pieces of cloth or leather. Female priests had additional responsibilities in the temples. They wove fabric and made clothing for the gods. They also cooked offerings of food for the deities.

Another important duty of priests was preserving the Aztecs' religious traditions. They were responsible for keeping the customs and beliefs of the Aztecs' ancestors alive. As the Aztecs explained to the Spanish, "From [our ancestors] we have inherited our pattern of life. . . . They taught us all their rules of worship, all their ways of honoring the gods."

The priests passed on this knowledge by instructing the calmecac students and by reciting speeches at public occasions to remind people how to live good lives. They also recorded the sacred teachings of their ancestors in books called codices. Made from folded strips of bark, these books were painted with images that told the ancient stories of the gods and of the Aztecs' origins. Other books made by priestly scribes were almanacs that documented the Aztecs' fascination with the passing of time.

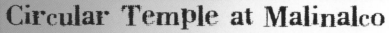

Circular Temple at Malinalco

On a hill high atop the present-day city of Malinalco sits a circular temple cut deep into the rock of the hillside, which is one of the greatest surviving Aztec monuments. The temple was built around 1486, about ten years after the area came under Aztec control. Thirteen steps led up to the temple's entrance, which is now shaded by a reconstructed, cone-shaped roof. Inside was a round chamber where warriors and nobles met to perform rituals. The cavelike space was decorated with beautiful stone carvings. A semicircular bench featured three carved seats. At the chamber's center stood a statue of an eagle. Next to it was a deep hole over which worshippers made blood offerings.

Keeping Time

The Aztecs had two calendars. One corresponded to the solar year, or the time it takes for the earth to revolve around the sun once. It included 365 days divided into 18 months of 20 days each. There were five days left over at the end the year. The Aztecs were cautious during these five transitional days, because they were considered to be unlucky.

Aztec priests performed a different ceremony each month. Otherwise, the 365-day calendar was used primarily to determine the proper days to plant and harvest crops. Spanish priest Diego Durán noted that farmers would not harvest ripe corn until first consulting with a priest: "They could have gathered the crop earlier, at their leisure; but since the old sorcerer found in his book or almanac that the day had come, he proclaimed it to the people, and they went off in great speed."

The other Aztec calendar, the **_tonalpohualli,_** was made up of 260 days. The name of each day included two parts, a day sign and a number between one and thirteen. There were twenty day

Playing for the Future

Aztec priests predicted the future in many ways, among them watching ball games. The Aztecs played ball in courts that had metal rings attached to two parallel walls. Using their hips and shoulders, players tried to bounce a hard rubber ball through one of the rings. If priests needed to determine the result of a future event, they assembled two teams and assigned a potential outcome to each. The priests believed the outcome assigned to the winning team would come true.

ma tlac tli Vn ey iz cuintli. q̃ quiere dzir. treze perrillos.

ce Vçu matli q̃ quiere. dezir Vna mona.

Vme malinali q̃ quiere dezir dos yeruas deste nonbre por q̃ tʒ çer quiere dezir malinale

yei acatl quiere dezir tres Cana

There were twenty different day signs in the tonalpohualli. These signs included, from left to right, dog, monkey, grass, and reed.

signs that were always counted off in the same order: Crocodile, Wind, House, Lizard, Serpent, Death, Deer, Rabbit, Water, Dog, Monkey, Grass, Reed, Jaguar, Eagle, Vulture, Movement, Flint, Rain, and Flower. In the calendar, 1 Crocodile was followed by 2 Wind, 3 House, and so, all the way up to 13 Reed. The number count then started over again with 1 Jaguar. Using this system, each day in a year had a unique name.

The days of the tonalpohualli guided the Aztecs throughout their lives. Using almanacs, priests interpreted each day as having a special meaning. They advised the Aztecs on the best day to do just about every activity, from traveling to getting married to holding festivals. Even the tlatoani consulted with priests to find out which days were the luckiest for conducting important matters of state.

When a baby was born, the parents asked a priest to interpret the meaning of his or her birthday. As Bernardino de Sahagún explained, "[The priest] looked at his books, at his paintings, his writings; he read, examined, looked at the day sign on which the baby was born, studied. . . . those related to it." Sometimes, the news was good. A child born on 5 Monkey, for instance, was fated to be well-liked. But in some cases, the interpretation was upsetting. For example, the life of a baby born on 6 Grass would be full of pain. To help offset a bad birthday, parents could wait to name their baby on a more advantageous day.

The End of the World

Priests also helped the Aztecs cope with a very dangerous time that occurred every fifty-two years, when the two Aztec calendars ended on the same day. The Aztecs feared that day could signal the end of the world. According to their ancient stories, at the end of time, earthquakes would shake the earth and great demons called the *Tzitzimime* would come from the sky and eat all human survivors.

In Tenochtitlán, people worked hard to prepare when the end of a fifty-two-year cycle approached. They frantically cleaned their homes, threw out their old clothes, and washed their statues of

Religion was an important part of every Aztec's life. Figures of gods and temples were often kept in household shrines.

the gods. On the cycle's final day, they put out their household fires, while priests extinguished the flames that burned in the temples. According to Bernardino de Sahagún, the Aztecs were filled with terror as the embers cooled. If the fires could not be relit, "then [the sun] would be destroyed forever; all would be ended; there would evermore be night."

At midnight, the residents of Tenochtitlán climbed to their rooftops and waited. On a high hill near the city, the powerful fire

priests set a new fire over the breast of a noble captive. When smoke rose over the hill, the Aztecs cheered as they realized the end had not come after all. Runners carried torches to other towns so that all the Aztecs' fires could be relit. Soon, everyone in the empire rejoiced at the news the runners brought: The priests, whose hard work kept their day-to-day lives in balance, had just saved the world.

Chapter IV

MERCHANTS AND CRAFTSPEOPLE

When Spanish soldier Bernal Díaz del Castillo visited the great Aztec market in the town of Tlatelolco, he was astounded by what he saw. He wished he could have written "of all the things which are sold there, but they are so numerous and of such different quality and the great market place with its surrounding arcade was so crowded with people, that one would not have been able to see and inquire about it all in two days." At Tlatelolco and other smaller markets, there was just about anything an Aztec could need or want. These markets were made possible by two of the most important groups of people in Aztec society. These were the craftspeople who made the goods and the merchants who bought and sold them.

The Pochteca

Many merchants worked within a small area. At local marketplaces, they sold items the Aztecs used every day, from bowls to baskets to sandals. They also offered a wide variety of foodstuffs, such as corn, fish, and turkeys. These local merchants generally obtained their wares from farming families living nearby.

Aztec merchants sometimes traveled by boat to conduct trade.

Some merchants, however, traveled great distances to trade in much more exotic goods. These men and women were called **pochteca**. Pochteca held a unique place among the Aztecs. They were commoners, but the most successful were as wealthy as nobles. These pochteca were so highly regarded that, for ceremonial occasions, they were allowed to wear cotton clothing, an honor otherwise jealously guarded by the noble class.

Not just anyone could become a pochteca. A pochteca had to inherit membership in one of the guilds, or trade organizations, that oversaw the business of all Aztec merchants. The pochteca also lived in their own neighborhoods, worshipped their own gods, and were governed by their own set of laws. When the merchants violated these laws, they were tried and sentenced in special pochteca-run courts instead of through the regular Aztec judicial system.

Many pochteca were hired by nobles, who told them what to buy on their behalf. For the most part, nobles wanted luxury items, such as gold jewelry, woven cloaks, and intricate stone carvings. These objects were emblems of the nobles' social standing. Wearing a beautiful garment or displaying an expensive piece of art told the rest of Aztec society that these nobles were worthy of respect.

A few pochteca worked directly for the tlatoani. The tlatoani Ahuitzotl, for instance, gave a pochteca 1,600 cotton garments to trade for shells, jade, and bird feathers. Ahuitzotl also provided the merchant with armed guards to protect him and his merchandise.

Trading Expeditions

To obtain the valuable objects their sponsors wanted, pochteca had to travel all over the empire. Organizing a trade **expedition** could take many months. Several pochteca and a few apprentice merchants usually traveled together. They were accompanied by *tlamama*, men employed to carry their merchandise. The Aztecs did not use vehicles to cart their goods. They instead relied on the tlamama, who wore large backpacks strapped to their foreheads. A tlamama could walk 15 miles (24 kilometers) a day carrying as much as 50 pounds (18.7 kilograms) of goods.

Before an expedition headed out, the lead pochteca in the traveling party held a ceremonial feast. During the ritual, the

The tlamama carried all of the merchants' goods on trade expeditions.

travelers washed their heads and cut their hair, which they would then let grow as long as their journey lasted. At the feast, older merchants lectured the younger ones about their duties and responsibilities. The pochteca also decorated walking sticks with paper to make them resemble fire gods. They believed these staffs would protect them from harm on the road.

Travelers had many things to fear. The pochteca had to hike over hills and mountains. A misstep could lead to a fatal accident. They also had to watch out for vicious wild animals. Even the people they met during their travels could pose a danger. Often, the pochteca journeyed to the edges of the empire through lands occupied by the Aztecs' enemies. If a pochteca were captured by enemy warriors, he could be jailed, tortured, or even killed.

Because expeditions took the pochteca into areas few other Aztecs cared to go, the tlatoani often enlisted their services as spies. Wearing the clothing and hairstyles of the enemy, the spies tried to blend into the local population. In disguise, they kept their eyes and ears open, learning everything they could about the enemy so they could give the tlatoani a complete report.

Back Home

The return of a pochteca expedition began a two-day ritual of feasting and speech making. The ceremony was meant to purify the traders. Their travels had exposed them to unfamiliar places and people. The homecoming ritual helped cleanse the pochteca of any dangerous powers they had brought back to the Aztecs' realm.

Elders questioned returning pochteca about every aspect of their trip. They also reminded the traders of their responsibilities, often reducing the pochteca to tears with their harsh words. The humbling of the pochteca was meant to remind them of their place in the social order. Coming back from a trading expedition, the pochteca stood to increase their wealth substantially. The elders wanted to make sure the pochteca remembered they were still commoners, inferior to the noble class no matter how rich they became.

Experienced pochteca were always careful not to display their wealth. As Spanish priest Bernardino de Sahagún noted, "They did not seek honor and fame." In fact, to hide their riches, they often made a point of returning from an expedition in the middle of the night. In the darkness, no one could see the treasures they brought home with them.

Shopping at Tlatelolco

Following an expedition, the pochteca distributed the goods promised to their noble sponsors. Anything they had left over was sold in marketplaces. Nearly every Aztec town held a market once every five days. Some regional merchants traveled from town to town, buying and selling goods at each market they visited. As a result, local markets were well stocked, though most commoners could only afford low-priced items such as locally grown foods, animals, and common household goods.

Women as well as men were sellers in these markets. Pictures in one codex show female merchants displaying many different goods. Among their offerings were capes, tamales, corn, beans, chili, salt, and tobacco. Some historical sources suggest that only poor women were involved in marketing.

The marketplaces in large cities had an even wider variety of merchandise. By far the biggest market was at Tlatelolco, an urban center on the outskirts of Tenochtitlán. The lakes surrounding Tenochtitlán were always full of canoes shipping goods to the Tlatelolco market.

Every day, the Tlatelolco marketplace attracted about 25,000 customers. Every fifth day, a special, bigger market was held. Then, as many as 60,000 people flocked to the city. As Bernal Díaz del Castillo wrote, "[O]ne could see every sort of merchandise that is to be found in the whole of New Spain." At Tlatelolco, customers could buy corn, tortillas, fish, eggs, vegetables, honey, and all kinds of game animals, from rabbits to deer. There were bricks, stones, and other building materials, as well as firewood, clothing, paint, and animal skins. For those with a fair amount of money to spend, there were beautiful ornaments made out of gold, silver, precious stones, shells, and even delicate bird feathers.

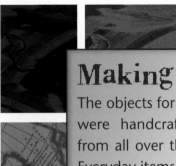

Making Art

The objects for sale at Tlatelolco were handcrafted by artisans from all over the Aztec Empire. Everyday items, such as cooking pots, knife blades, and sandals, were usually made by craftspeople working at home. Often, farmers made these wares in their free time to earn extra income.

Order in the Marketplace

Tlatelolco was more than just a place to shop. At the marketplace, people could visit with neighbors and hear the latest news. Often, customers made new friends or met possible mates. The social aspect of marketing was clear to Diego Durán, a Spanish priest who visited Tlatelolco. He wrote, "The markets are so inviting, pleasurable, appealing, and gratifying to these people that great crowds attended."

Given the size of the crowds at Tlatelolco, the marketplace was amazingly well organized. Pochteca were in charge of overseeing the markets. They appointed officials to police the grounds. These officials set prices for goods and divided the marketplace into sections. In each section, a different type of merchandise was sold.

The officials also kept their eyes out for thieves. A common scam involved the seeds of the cacao tree, which were often used as money. Dishonest customers and merchants removed the outer skin of these seeds and filled them with sawdust. Anyone caught using counterfeit seeds was severely punished. As Hernán Cortés explained in a letter to Charles I, the king of Spain, "[At Tlatelolco] there is . . . a very large building like a

Modern-era painting imagines what an Aztec marketplace looked like in the city of Tenochtitlan.

courthouse, where ten or twelve persons sit as judges. They preside over all that happens in the market, and sentence criminals."

However, luxury items, such as feathered fans and gold jewelry, were usually made by full-time professional craftspeople. They worked alongside other artisans in workshops specializing in one craft technique. Artisans generally lived in urban areas, clustered in their own neighborhoods. Some worked directly for nobles, making pieces to their sponsors' specifications. Because their wares helped nobles maintain their privileged status, artisans had a good deal of influence within the Aztec Empire. For instance, a group of gem cutters once convinced the tlatoani Motecuhzoma II to conquer several towns that had a supply of sand the artisans needed to polish precious stones.

The Spanish were in awe of the work produced by the Aztecs. Hernán Cortés wrote the Spanish king that none of "the princes of this world, of whom we know, possess any things of such high quality." The Spanish were most interested in Aztec items made of gold, but Cortés admitted that other art objects were "so marvelous

Aztec Figurines

At many Aztec sites, archaeologists have found small clay figurines, many of which represented women. These sculptures, each about 4 to 8 inches (10 to 20 centimeters) tall, were likely made by professional craftspeople for use in the home. Scholars, though, are not sure what the figurines' functions were. They may have been part of household shrines or possibly gifts given to small children to protect them from illness and evil.

Song and Dance

According to Spanish sources, the Aztecs loved to sing and dance. Although dancing was usually part of religious ceremonies, it was also a form of entertainment. Men and women danced together in a circle around musicians playing drums, clay flutes, shell trumpets, and rattles. Nobles often had skilled composers among their attendants. Whenever there was a war victory, marriage, or other special occasion, the composers were asked to write original songs for the celebration.

that considering their novelty and strangeness, they are priceless." As an example, he sent Charles I a spectacular headdress crafted from brilliantly colored green and blue feathers.

Beautiful Objects

To the Aztecs, feather working was the most honored craft. Highly trained artisans carefully glued and tied fragile feathers together to create shields, cloaks, and fans. Sometimes they used feathers from ducks and turkeys dyed in different colors. But the most valuable feather objects were made from the colorful feathers of exotic birds, such as parrots and macaws. Particularly treasured were the long, green tail feathers of the quetzal, a bird native to what is now Guatemala. Quetzal feathers were one of the many types of raw art materials that the pochteca brought to the Aztec capital.

The Aztecs were also experts at stoneworking, their oldest craft tradition. Using blades and drills, they carved slightly raised images into huge stones. They also made large sculptures, which were often displayed outside of temples.

Smaller ornamental items were often adorned with mosaics. Mosaic artisans glued together small pieces of turquoise, shell, and precious stones to form intricate designs. Mosaics were used to decorate sculptures, knife handles, and even human skulls.

Precious stones were also used to make jewelry. Both beautiful and rare, jade was prized above all other stones by the Aztecs. It was most often used to make beaded necklaces. Other ornaments worn by Aztec nobles, including rings, pendants, and earrings, were cast from gold. The Aztecs probably learned about metalworking from Indian peoples to the south, especially the Mixtecs. In fact, some of the goldworkers in Tenochtitlán may have been Mixtec immigrants. After invading the Aztec Empire, the Spanish melted down most of the Aztecs' beautiful gold objects. But, before their destruction, even Cortés had to admire the Aztecs' craftsmanship. As he wrote to the Spanish king, "No smith in the world could have done better."

Otumba

Scholars studying the Aztecs used to think that most craftspeople worked in Tenochtitlán. But in the late 1980s, the excavation of Otumba proved them wrong. In this town a team of archaeologists found the remains of craft goods, including obsidian blades, figurines, and pottery. They discovered so many ornament fragments made from precious stones that they were able to document how Aztec craftspeople made these goods from start to finish.

Each type of craft item found at Otumba was concentrated in a specific area. This fact told the archaeologists that specialists in certain crafts labored together in small workshops located in or near their houses. The large number of goods found at Otumba also suggests that the goods may have been made for export to other cities.

Chapter V

FARMERS

"The farmer . . . is bound to the soil; he works—works the soil, stirs the soil anew, prepares the soil; he weeds, breaks up the clods, hoes, . . . he plants, hills, waters." With these words, Spanish priest Bernardino de Sahagún described the endless work of Aztecs who made their living off the land. Farmers were on the lower rungs of Aztec society, yet it was their labor above all that made the Aztec civilization possible. The food they grew sustained an enormous population, allowing the upper classes to expand the Aztecs' empire and power.

Growing Corn

By the sixteenth century, about one million people lived in the Valley of Mexico, while some two to three million lived in the surrounding valleys. Most of the Aztecs living in the countryside were farmers. Using basic farming tools, including a wooden digging stick called a *coa*, they cleared and tended small plots. After feeding their families, farmers used surplus crops to trade with neighbors for other goods and to pay tribute to the tlatoani.

Farming families grew an assortment of fruits, vegetables, and herbs. But by far, their most important crop was corn. Corn grew well in nearly every part of Mesoamerica, where it had been cultivated for thousands of years. Drawing on the farming know-how of their ancestors, Aztec

The Aztecs used simple tools in farming their lands. Corn was their most important crop.

farmers produced large corn crops, making it their principal source of food.

Reflecting the crop's importance in their lives, the Aztecs worshipped several corn gods. Xilonen protected the green ears when they first sprouted. Centéotl guarded the corn as it ripened. The Aztecs praised Chicomecoatl, the most significant corn goddess, as "our sustenance . . . . our flesh, our livelihood."

A Varied Diet

After corn, the most significant crop for the Aztecs was beans. According to Sahagún, farmers grew "yellow beans, white ones, black, red, pinto beans, [and] large beans." Eaten with corn, beans gave the Aztecs a desperately needed source of protein. Although the Aztecs raised dogs, turkeys, and ducks for food, meat was a fairly small part of their diet.

Other vegetables farmed by the Aztecs included tomatoes, avocados, onions, squash, and chili peppers. Between corn harvests, they also relied on the amaranth plant, as its seeds could replace corn in many of their favorite foods. Aztec priests also used amaranth seeds to make dough that they molded into figurines depicting the gods.

With mild disgust, several Spaniards noted that the Aztecs ate insects. The Aztecs considered ants, grasshoppers, and worms, when cooked properly, to be a tasty treat. They also enjoyed cakes made from algae, which fishers skimmed off the surfaces of lakes. Bernal Díaz del Castillo wrote that the algae "curdles and forms a kind of bread which tastes rather like cheese."

Another important Aztec crop was the maguey cactus. In areas with too little rain to grow corn, Aztec farmers planted maguey, which required far less water. Out of the sap of the maguey leaves, the Aztecs made **pulque**, a fermented alcoholic drink that nobles drank during ceremonies. Drinking too much pulque, however, was against Aztec law.

Maguey provided the Aztecs with the materials needed to make many necessities. In fact, Spanish priest Toribio de Benavente wrote that "as many things are made of it as are said to be made of

Aztec farmers made a drink out of maguey cactus.

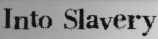

Into Slavery

Between 1450 and 1454, a long period of drought led to starvation throughout the Aztec world. In order to survive, many poor Aztecs had to sell themselves into slavery. As slaves, they worked for no pay, but their owners were required to feed and cloth them. Slaves could eventually escape their situation by buying their freedom. Many people, therefore, saw slavery as a temporary state. They entered slavery when times were bad, hoping to free themselves when things improved.

iron." Fibers pulled from maguey leaves could be used as thread or twisted into rope. Weaving the fibers together, Aztec women made fabric for the clothing worn by commoners. The spines of the leaves served as sewing needles, while the plant's thorns made excellent nails. Maguey thorns also played an important role in Aztec religious life, because people used them pierce their flesh during bloodletting rituals.

More Mouths to Feed

Thousands of Aztec farmers in the countryside worked the land much as their ancestors had. But as the Aztec Empire grew, feeding the increasing population became more difficult using the old methods alone. By the fifteenth century, just a few years of low rainfall could bring on a devastating famine.

As the Aztec population grew, several tlatoque waged war specifically to obtain more farmland. They also conquered foreign peoples in order to obtain foodstuffs in the form of tribute. At the same time, farmers worked to increase the food supply by developing new techniques to bring the highest yields possible from the least amount of land. They also discovered ways to grow crops in areas previously thought to be unfarmable.

Irrigation was used along river valleys throughout the Aztec Empire. By digging canals, farmers diverted water from small rivers and springs to dry farmland. Older Indian civilizations had used irrigation, but the Aztecs built bigger and better canals, making the system a far more effective way to keep fertile farmlands well watered.

Another widespread agricultural method was terrace farming. Much of what is now central Mexico is mountainous. The Aztecs learned to cut into sloping hillsides to make flat planting surfaces. To keep dirt from the hillside from falling into these farming plots, the Aztecs constructed miles of stone walls. The remains of some of these stone walls can still be seen in Mexico today.

Chinampa Farming

An even more ingenious farming innovation was *chinampa* farming. Chinampas were artificial islands of farmland the Aztecs built in the lakes surrounding Tenochtitlán. Each chinampa plot was about 33 yards (30 m) long and 2.7 yards (2.5 m) wide. To construct a chinampa, farmers drove stakes into a lake bed to form a rectangle. They then filled the space inside with vegetation and mud scraped from the bottom of the lake. Farmers built rows and rows of plots, carefully leaving a canal between each. They also planted willow trees along the edges of the fields. The long roots of the willow helped to hold the soil in place.

Building and maintaining chinampas was hard work. Working from canoes, farmers planted and tended the plots. Frequently, they had to enrich the chinampas' soil with more nutrient-rich mud dug up from lake bottoms. Using dams, farmers also had to

regulate the water level carefully so that the plots never became too wet or too dry. Even the willows needed constant tending. Farmers had to trim their leaves regularly to keep them from blocking sunlight from the growing plants.

Chinampa farming, however, was worth the effort. The plots were extremely fertile. They could produce three or four crops a year. Particularly productive were the chinampas of the farming towns of Xochimilco, Chalco, and Cuitláhuac, just south of Tenochtitlán. These towns provided as much as half the food eaten by Tenochtitlán's 200,000 residents.

Pleasure Gardens

Most Aztec farmers, whether tending rural fields or urban chinampas, were consumed with planting, hoeing, weeding, and other day-to-day chores. There was, however, a small group of farmers who devoted themselves to learning how to grow exotic plants from far-flung regions of the empire. These farmers were responsible for the botanical gardens of the Aztec elite.

One botanical garden was established in the town of Huaxtepec. When Motecuhzoma I was the tlatoani, the remains of an ancient garden were discovered there. Motecuhzoma hired a farmer named Pinotetl to

A modern-day painting depicts the construction of chinampas, a type of floating farm.

rebuild the garden's grounds and fountains. Pinotetl was assisted by farmers from the coast of the Gulf of Mexico. On Motecuhzoma's orders, messengers brought these farmers, along with specimens of several tropical plants, to Huaxtepec. Soon, the royal garden was blooming with vanilla orchids and cacao trees.

While marching toward Tenochtitlán, Spanish leader Hernán Cortés visited another pleasure garden at a noble's house in Ixtappalapan. He later wrote Spain's king, Charles I, about its "many trees and sweet-scented flowers, [and] bathing places of fresh water." Cortés was equally impressed by the home's orchards, which featured "a walk with a well-laid pavement of tiles, so wide that four persons can walk abreast on it" and a "pool contain[ing] many fish and different kinds of waterfowl." Like the farmers of the countryside, the gardeners of Ixtappalapan worked with nature to transform the earth and make it bloom.

Chapter VI

HOUSEKEEPERS, COOKS, AND WEAVERS

The Spaniards who first studied the Aztecs wrote extensively about their warriors, priests, and merchants. Most people in these positions were men. The Spaniards, on the other hand, had little interest in the labor performed within the homes of average Aztec families. This was in large part because of the Spaniards' disregard for women, who oversaw household work. The Aztecs, however, understood how vital women's work was to their society and their empire. From her earliest days, an Aztec woman was instructed in her responsibilities and praised for her hard work in the home. Indeed, among the first words a baby girl heard was the declaration, "You will be the heart of the house."

Keeping House

Most Aztecs lived in relatively modest houses made up of one or more rooms that opened onto an outdoor patio. Still, a woman was expected to keep this small space very clean. It was especially important that she make sure its earth floors were frequently swept. Women were expected to wake up at dawn to begin their sweeping.

The act of sweeping held great meaning to the Aztecs. This is clear from the gifts given to Aztec children. Young boys received miniature shields and arrows, symbols of the importance their role as future warriors was to their society. Young girls, on the other hand, received small brooms. These, too, were symbols of a woman's most significant contribution to her people. In the Aztecs' minds, sweeping was a means of protecting themselves from the chaos that always threatened order in the world.

Sweeping seemed to have had religious meaning to the Aztecs. It was an important part of priests' diligent maintenance of the temples. Just as they swept to protect the temples from disorder, women swept their homes to keep their families safe from harm. Many rules and rituals were associated with household sweeping. Brooms were always stored outside to keep them from contaminating the house. For the same reason, children were told never to play with brooms.

When a woman's husband went to war, she increased the time she spent sweeping. She also devoted more attention to another of her household duties, making daily offerings to the gods. Within the home, women sought to please the gods by burning incense and offering them food or even the women's own blood. In wartime, while making their offerings, they prayed for their husbands' safe return. To aid their warrior husbands, they also took out the thighbones of killed captives that their spouses had seized in earlier conflicts. During a ritual, women wrapped the bones in paper and hung them from the house beams.

Food for the Household

The most sacred part of an Aztec house was its hearth. There, a fire continually burned. Working over the flames, women performed another vital task, cooking the meals their families ate. All women were expected to be good cooks. Even the daughters of rulers were instructed to "look well to the drink, to the food: how it is prepared, how it is made."

Corn was by far the Aztecs' most important source of food. Women made a dough out of most of the corn harvested. They first boiled the kernels in a large pot. Before placing the corn in the hot water, women made a point of warming it with their breath so that the corn would not fear the water's heat.

After draining the boiled corn, they ground it on a **metate**, or grinding stone. Metates were treated with great care. The Aztecs believed that if one broke while a woman was using it, she or a

A later illustration shows Aztec women making corn tortillas, which were an important part of the Aztec diet.

Quachtli

In addition to cacao beans, *quachtli* were used as currency in Aztec marketplaces. Quachtli were capes sewn from cotton cloth. Anyone could weave quachtli, but wearing one was an honor reserved for nobles. The worth of quachtli depended on their quality. One could be bought for anywhere from sixty-five to three hundred cacao beans. The Aztecs generally used quachtli to make large purchases. For instance, it might take six hundred quachtli to buy a particularly fine jade necklace.

member of her household would die. Grinding corn on a metate was hard, time-consuming work. A woman might spend as many as eight hours a day grinding corn for her family.

Corn formed the base of many delicious dishes. At nearly every meal, the Aztecs enjoyed tortillas. Women made these flat, round pieces of bread by patting dough into thin sheets and cooking them on a clay griddle. The Aztecs often covered tortillas with tasty sauces flavored with chili peppers, ground gourd seeds, and tomatoes. Because tortillas could be stored easily, they were a favorite food of travelers.

The Aztecs also ate sweet and spicy meat-stuffed tamales. Though delicious, tamales took a long time to make. Commoners ate them only on ritual occasions. Then, women of the household sometimes stayed up all night working the dough. Nobles ate tamales more often, because they had female kitchen staffs at their beck and call. Another popular Aztec dish was *atole*, a thin soup flavored with chilis or fruit. The Aztecs often sipped atole at breakfast, because they believed it had medicinal powers that would protect them from illness for the rest of the day.

Weavers and Weaving

The food Aztec women cooked helped their population to grow and their people to prosper. But another women's job, weaving, had just as much impact on the Aztec economy. The cloth and clothing they made was essential to the well being of their empire.

Mothers passed along their knowledge of weaving to their daughters, inspiring them with gifts of miniature spinning wheels and weaving tools. Girls as young as three years learned to spin

Aztec weavers produced beautiful cloth with interesting designs, such as the cloth shown here.

thread. They used simple spindles weighted down with clay disks called **whorls**. Archaeologists have found spindle whorls throughout Aztec territory. This suggests that just about everywhere in the empire, women spent time weaving. It was considered important work for female commoners and nobles alike.

The Aztecs spun thread from materials of two plants, maguey and cotton. Thread made from the fibers of maguey leaves generally produced a coarse cloth. Commoners wore clothing made from maguey, but nobles much preferred soft cotton cloth against their skin.

At about age thirteen, young women began weaving the thread they had spun into cloth. They used large looms to make cloth for clothing, bags, bedding, and decorative hangings. Sometimes, they colored the cloth with dyes made by boiling plants and insects.

The cloth women made had several purposes. Some they sewed into their families' clothing. Many woman also used cloth to pay tribute to the ruler. Cloth made in women's houses sometimes ended up for sale in markets. It is uncertain whether this cloth was originally tribute or whether women made cloth specifically for sale. It is clear, though, that a skilled weaver helped her family to prosper. This talent was in fact so important that one could not be a good Aztec woman without being a good weaver as well.

THE LEGACY
OF THE
ANCIENT AZTECS

"Who could conquer Tenochtitlán? Who could shake the foundation of the heavens?" When an Aztec poet asked these questions, it seemed impossible that there could be an answer. In the early sixteenth century, the Aztec Empire was large and powerful. Certainly, to those under the tlatoani's rule, the end of the great Aztec capital could scarcely be imagined.

But in 1521, Tenochtitlán came under attack from a foreign enemy. Within months, its great palaces and temples were destroyed. Many thousands of its people were slaughtered. The once glorious Tenochtitlán lay in ruins, and the Aztec Empire was gone forever.

Strangers from the Sea

The story of Tenochtitlán's destruction began in February 1519. To the east of the city, five hundred Spanish soldiers in eleven ships arrived on the coast of the Gulf of Mexico. The soldiers were commanded by Hernán Cortés. His ships had sailed from present-day Cuba, where the Spanish had established a military base. At the last minute, the Spanish governor in Cuba tried to cancel

Cortés's expedition. But Cortés ignored the orders and set sail anyway.

At the time, the Aztec tlatoani was Motecuhzoma II. Motecuhzoma began his reign in 1502. Over the next seventeen years, he proved to be a skillful leader. One codex recorded that "his subjects greatly respected him because of his gravity, demeanor, and power; none of his predecessors, in comparison, could approach his great state and majesty."

Traveling up the coast, the Spanish had their first contact with the Aztecs at the town of Cempoala. When Motecuhzoma heard about these strange men in his realm, he sent ambassadors bearing gifts to meet them. The Spanish soldiers were thrilled by these tokens, especially by several beautiful items made of gold. Aztec nobles later told Bernardino de Sahagún about the Spaniards' fevered reaction: "Like monkeys they seized upon the gold. . . . For in truth they thirsted mightily for gold; they stuffed themselves with it, and starved and lusted for it like pigs."

Cortés took the ambassadors captive and made them watch his men fire a cannon. The ambassadors were terrified. No Aztec had ever seen such a loud and deadly weapon. Cortés then set the ambassadors

The arrival of Cortés would change the Aztecs forever.

free and sent them back to Tenochtitlán, so they could tell Motecuhzoma what they had seen.

Building an Army

The Cempoalans were also awed by the soldiers' guns and steel
swords, European weapons they had never encountered before.
But they were even more impressed by Cortés's boldness. When
Cortés heard the Cempoalans complaining about paying tribute,
he convinced them to imprison several of Motecuhzoma's hated
tax collectors. The Cempoalans were inspired by Cortés's willingness to stand up to these powerful men.

This show of strength was part of Cortés's strategy for dealing
with the Aztecs. He saw that on the outskirts of the empire many

people were angry at the tlatoani. They were tired of paying tribute, but too frightened of Motecuhzoma to stop. Cortés heard about the riches in Tenochtitlán but knew he could not take the city with his small army alone. But if he could convince the Cempoalans and other discontented people under Aztec rule to rebel, he had a chance of defeating even the mighty Motecuhzoma.

After forming an alliance with the Cempoalans, Cortés's men moved inland to Tlaxcala. Bolstered by Cempoalan warriors, the Spanish army engaged the Tlaxcalans in several bloody battles before Cortés persuaded them to join him in overtaking Tenochtitlán. With a growing force of Indian allies, the Spanish continued on to the holy city of Cholula. The nobles of Cholula greeted the Spanish, but the Tlaxcalans convinced Cortés that they were planning a surprise attack. Cortés decided to strike first. In the courtyard of the town's main temple, his army slaughtered about five thousand unarmed Cholula warriors. Cortés's men then looted the city.

Motecuhzoma's Strategy

News of the massacre quickly reached Tenochtitlán, but Motecuhzoma did nothing to stop Cortés's approach. Perhaps the tlatoani did not believe the Spanish planned to invade the city. After all, in Aztec custom, an invading army warned an enemy of the date and place it would attack. Cortés made no such warning; instead, he sent messages extending friendship to Motecuhzoma.

Aztec nobles later gave Spanish priests another explanation for Motecuhzoma's unwillingness to act. They said that Motecuhzoma thought Cortés was Quetzalcoatl, a figure in both Aztec history and religion. Quetzalcoatl was one of the most important Aztec gods. He was also a Toltec ruler who, according to Aztec myth, pledged to return and rule again one day. Quetzalcoatl made his vow in the Aztec year 1 Reed. That year name was also given to 1519. Therefore, the nobles said, Motecuhzoma believed Cortés was the legendary Quetzalcoatl coming back to fulfill his promise.

Some modern scholars, however, question this account. They suspect that the nobles were embarrassed by Motecuhzoma's behavior. The story of Motecuhzoma mistaking Cortés for a god was perhaps a way of covering up the fact that their great tlatoani had made a fatal military error by underestimating the Spanish and their Indian allies.

Friends or Enemies?

When Cortés's army reached the edge of Tenochtitlán, enormous crowds gathered to get a look at them. Spanish lieutenant Bernal Díaz del Castillo later wrote, "Who could count the multitude of men, women, and boys in the streets, on the roof-tops and in canoes on the waterways, who had come out to see us?"

Motecuhzoma soon emerged from his palace, walking through the crowd to greet the Spanish leader. Spanish priest Diego Durán described the momentous meeting: "[Cortés] went to embrace the Aztec sovereign, treating him with much reverence. Motecuhzoma did the same, paying homage to the other with humility and words of welcome. From one of his noblemen he took a splendid necklace of gold, inlaid with precious stones, and placed it around Cortés's neck."

For the next few days, Motecuhzoma put the Spaniards up in his father's luxurious palace. He gave them a tour of Tenochtitlán, showing off its awesome pyramid temples and bustling marketplace. Cortés returned Motecuhzoma's hospitality by taking him hostage. Many of Motecuhzoma's noble attendants

Motecuhzoma met Cortés and treated him kindly. Despite the warm welcome, Cortés took Motecuhzoma captive.

tried to flee as Cortés seized control of Tenochtitlán, and the Spanish began to pillage its treasures.

The Battle for Tenochtitlán

For several months, Cortés ruled over the Aztec capital. Then suddenly, the Spanish commander left Tenochtitlán. Hearing that Spanish soldiers were coming to arrest him for disobeying the orders of the Cuban governor, Cortés headed to the coast to confront them.

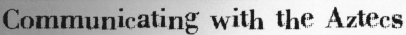

Communicating with the Aztecs

To speak with the Aztecs, Cortés had to rely on two translators. One was a Spaniard named Gerónimo de Aguilar. He had been living among the Maya Indians for eight years after he was shipwrecked during an ill-fated Spanish expedition. The second translator was La Malinche. She was a noble-woman who was taken captive by the Maya and given to Cortés as a battle prize. Cortés spoke to Aguilar in Spanish. Aguilar then translated his words into Maya for La Malinche. She then repeated them in Nahuatl, the language of the Aztecs, for Cortés's Aztec audience.

Before leaving, Cortés put Pedro Alvarado in charge of Tenochtitlán. Under Alvarado's command, the Spanish army turned brutal. During a ceremony to honor the Aztec god Huitzilopochtli, Alvarado's soldiers attacked a group of warriors while they danced. The warriors fought back, and the entire city became a battleground.

Meanwhile, Cortés pacified the Spanish force on the coast and headed back to Tenochtitlán. His men fought their way back into the capital. During the chaos, Motecuhzoma was killed, possibly by the Spanish. Some scholars, however, think he died at the hands of Aztecs who were outraged that he had allowed Cortés to enter the city. Taking over as tlatoani, Motecuhzoma's brother Cuitláhuac rallied the Aztec army to crush the invaders.

Cortés soon realized his men were overwhelmed by the Aztec fighting force. On the night of June 30, 1520, he ordered them

Fighting between the Spanish and Aztec warriors broke out during a ceremony to honor the god Huitzilopochtli.

to retreat from the city. Their progress was slow, because the Spanish were weighted down with looted gold. As they scurried down the western road out of Tenochtitlán, Cuitláhuac's warriors attacked. Five hundred Spaniards and two thousand of their Indian allies were killed. Because of the massive casualties, the botched retreat was later called *La Noche Triste*, meaning "Night of Sadness."

Disease and Death

About four hundred Spaniards, including Cortés, survived the massacre. They fled to Tlaxcala, where they stayed for five months, recovering from their wounds and waiting for reinforcements. At the same time, the victorious Aztecs were dealt a devastating blow. Unknowingly, the Spanish had infected the people of Tenochtitlán with smallpox. The Aztecs had never before been exposed to this European disease and therefore had no natural immunity to it.

Tenochtitlán was soon in the grip of an epidemic. The victims of smallpox suffered horribly. Painful sores erupted all over their bodies before the disease killed them. Those who did not fall to smallpox were faced with a massive famine. Many people who were uninfected died of starvation.

Within three months, Tenochtitlán was littered with corpses. About half of the city's population had died. Among the victims was Cuitláhuac. Leadership of the Aztecs then fell to Motecuhzoma's nephew Cuauhtémoc, who was known as a fearless warrior.

An Empire Destroyed

While smallpox was still ravaging Tenochtitlán, Cortés's army returned, bolstered by thousands of Indian warriors. As the soldiers and warriors marched on the Aztec capital, they were shocked by what they saw. Even Cortés was moved. He later wrote to the Spanish king of the horror the epidemic had caused: "Indeed, so great was their suffering that it was beyond our understanding how they could endure it."

Yet Cortés did not hesitate to add to the Aztecs' misery. For three months, his men relentlessly battled the survivors. The Spaniards leveled the city, house by house, in order to prevent its Aztec defenders from firing darts and arrows down from the rooftops. Spanish boats blocked the canals surrounding Tenochtitlán so that no food could reach the city. The starving Aztecs fought bravely, but their weapons were no match for the Spaniards' guns and cannons.

On August 13, 1521, the Spanish took Cuauhtémoc hostage. The capture of the tlatoani effectively ended the Aztecs' defense of their city. The Spaniards overran Tenochtitlán, destroying its great palaces, plazas, and temples. They slaughtered innocent Aztecs and looted their victims' homes, reducing them to rubble. Bernal Díaz del Castillo wrote, "[T]oday all lies overthrown, and lost, nothing left standing."

With the fall of Tenochtitlán, the Aztec Empire came to an end. For centuries, students of the Aztecs have marveled that the greatest empire in North America could have been crushed so quickly, especially given the small size of the Spanish force. In fact, their victory is hardly surprising when several factors are considered. The superior weaponry of the Spanish in part explains their victory. So does their unintentional unleashing of disease, which destroyed much of the Tenochtitlán's population before the final battle even began. But also central to understanding the empire's defeat is that fact that it faced not only an invasion by foreigners, but also an internal revolt. Cortés's army

yepolinhą mexica

The capture
of Cuauhtémoc
meant the end
of Tenochtitlán.

most likely could never have taken Tenochtitlán without the help
of disgruntled Aztec subjects. The Aztec leadership, therefore,
contributed to its own demise by inspiring the spirit of rebellion
among its people.

A Spanish Colony

After Tenochtitlán's destruction, ships full of Spanish colonists
headed for the land of the Aztecs. They set about rebuilding the
capital, constructing churches where temples had once stood. In

time, Tenochtitlán was reborn as Mexico City, and the Aztecs' realm became part of New Spain.

Under Spanish rule, many Indians were forced to work on farms and in mines. At the same time, they were plagued with new epidemics of European diseases, such as measles and typhus. Hard labor and disease took a devastating toll on the Indian population. By 1580, only about 200,000 Indians were living in the Valley of Mexico, just one-fifth the number of the people in the area when Cortés first arrived.

A few Aztec nobles found a place in the Spanish ruling class. But for the most part, the privileged way of life enjoyed by the nobles was destroyed with the Spanish conquest. In the countryside, however, farmers and craftspeople labored much as they had in the past. They were now ruled by Spanish overlords instead of by local Aztec leaders and the tlatoani, but otherwise their day-to-day lives remained largely unchanged, with one exception. Immediately after the Spanish took power, they began trying to convert Indians to their own religion, Catholicism. Under intense pressure from Spanish priests, most Indians became Catholics, though they continued to worship their own gods. Over time, these Indian converts developed their own unique brand of Catholicism.

The story of the Virgin of Guadalupe illustrates this blending of European and Indian traditions. In 1531, just ten years after the fall of Tenochtitlán, a poor Indian named Juan Diego saw a vision of the Virgin Mary on the hill of Tepeyac. For the Aztecs, the hill had been a sacred site dedicated to the worship of the sacred mother goddess Tonantzin. In Diego's vision, Mary was dark-skinned and spoke Nahuatl, the Aztec language. When Diego told local priests what he had seen, at first they did not believe him, claiming that Mary would never reveal herself to a common

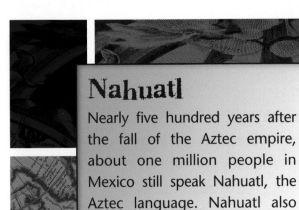

Nahuatl

Nearly five hundred years after the fall of the Aztec empire, about one million people in Mexico still speak Nahuatl, the Aztec language. Nahuatl also lives on in several words adopted by English speakers. For instance, *tomato*, *avocado*, and *chocolate* come from the Nahuatl words *tomatl*, *ahuacatl*, and *chocolatl*.

Indian. But the church eventually accepted the vision as a miracle. Tepeyac is now the site of great church that is visited by millions of Catholics each year.

The Aztecs in Modern Mexico

Today, Mexico is a modern country, and Mexico City is a modern national capital. But in many ways, the Aztec past is still seen and felt in everyday life there. The most obvious Aztec influence is the food Mexicans eat every day. Corn and beans remain staples of the Mexican diet. Other crops grown by the Aztecs, including avocados, chilies, and squash, are also common ingredients in Mexican cooking.

Outdoor markets are almost as popular with today's Mexicans as they were with the Aztecs. Most large cities and towns have at least one daily market, while smaller neighborhoods host a market once a week. Wares on sale include pottery and cloth made using techniques developed by the ancient Aztecs.

Throughout Mexico City, public and government buildings are adorned with beautiful murals depicting Aztec life. Many are the works of Diego Rivera, one of Mexico's greatest artists. In the mid-twentieth century, he painted many murals celebrating the achievements and spirituality of the Aztec civilization.

For further evidence of their Aztec past, Mexicans only have to look at their nation's flag. Adopted in 1821, it features horizontal stripes of green, white, and red, representing independence, religion, and unity. In the center of the white stripe is an eagle standing on a cactus with a snake in its mouth. The image recalls the story of the early Aztecs' arrival in the land they were destined to rule. It reminds Mexicans of the twenty-first century that they are heirs to the legacy of the once mighty Aztecs.

The legacy of the Aztecs can be seen today on the Mexican flag.

Time Line

The ancient city of
Teotihuacán flourishes.

| 6,500 B.C.–2,000 B.C. | 150 B.C.–A.D. 750 | C. 900–1150 |

Farmers begin growing
corn, beans, and squash
in present-day Mexico.

The Toltec
Empire is at its
height.

The Mexica settle in the Valley of Mexico at the site of the future city of Tenochtitlán.

The tlatonai Itzcoatl negotiates the Triple Alliance, marking the beginning of Aztec dominance in the Valley of Mexico.

1325

1375

1426

1450–1454

Acamapichtli becomes the first tlatoani of the Aztecs.

The Aztecs suffer from famine after years of low rainfall.

Spanish soldiers led by Hernán Cortés arrive on what is now the Gulf Coast of Mexico in February. Cortés arrives in Tenochtitlán on November 8.

Cuauhtémoc, the last Aztec tlatoani, is captured on August 13, signaling the end of armed Aztec resistance to the Spanish invasion.

1502	1519	1520	1521	1531

Motecuhzoma II begins his reign as tlatoani.

Hundreds of Spanish soldiers are driven from Tenochtitlán on La Noche Triste on June 30.

Juan Diego sees a vision of the Virgin Mary at Tepeyac.

The Stone of the Sun, also known as the Aztec Calendar Stone, is unearthed in Mexico City.

The disk of Coyolxauhqui is discovered in downtown Mexico City.

1790   **1821**   **1978**   **1978–present**

Mexico wins its independence from Spain.

The ruins of the Templo Mayor are excavated.

Acamapichtli

Acamapichtli, meaning "Handful of Arrows," was the first tlatoani of the Aztecs, reigning from 1375 to 1395. According to Aztec myth, fifty-two years after the Mexicas arrived in the Valley of Mexico, they asked the leader of the nearby Culhuas for a ruler to guide them. The Culhua leader named Acamapichtli, his daughter's son. Acamapichtli's father was an Aztec noblemen, so within him the Culhua and Mexica bloodlines merged. The Culhuas were said to be descended from the great Toltecs, so Acamapichtli could claim ancestry from the Toltecs as well.

Ahuitzotl

While still in school, the young Ahuitzotl was selected to serve as tlatoani after the death of his brother Tizoc, possibly at the hands of his own attendants. Ruling from 1486 to 1503, Ahuitzotl, a grandson of Motecuhzoma I, waged several successful wars that expanded the empire from coast to coast. He also renovated the Templo Mayor, the great temple complex in the center of Tenochtitlán. At its dedication, at least twenty thousand war captives were sacrificed.

Axayacatl

A grandson of Motecuhzoma I, Axayacatl ruled the Aztecs between 1469 and 1481. Like Motecuhzoma I, he greatly expanded the Aztec empire through military conquest. During his reign, the Aztecs defeated Tlatelolco, the great market city that became an important source of food and goods for Tenochtitlán. Later campaigns of Axayacatl, however, were less successful. He experienced a particularly humiliating defeat at the hands of the Tarascans to the west.

Fernando de Alva Ixtlilxóchitl

Born in 1578, Alva Ixtlilxóchitl wrote Spanish-language histories of the expansion of the Aztec Empire. Of mixed Indian and Spanish ancestry, he was a descendant of Ixtlilxóchitl, who ruled the Aztec city of Texcoco from 1409 to 1418. Alva Ixtlilxóchitl was educated at the Colegio de Santa Cruz, which was operated by the Spanish priest and historian Bernardino de Sahagún. Alva Ixtlilxóchitl died in 1650.

Cuauhtémoc

Born in Tenochtitlán in about 1496, Cuauhtémoc was the son of Ahuitzotl and reigned as the Aztec tlatoani from 1520 to 1525. After attending the calmacac, Cuauhtémoc distinguished himself on the battlefield. In 1521, Cuauhtémoc became tlatoani after the death of his uncle Cuitláhuac during an epidemic. He valiantly defended Tenochtitlán from invasion by a Spanish and Indian force led by Hernán Cortés. As the city fell, the Spanish captured Cuauhtémoc. He was subsequently tortured and hanged in 1525 when the Spanish suspected him of inciting a rebellion.

Cuitláhuac

After Motecuhzoma II's death in battle in 1520, his brother Cuitláhuac became tlatoani. During his reign, the Aztecs continued to resist the Spanish. In June, his warriors drove the Spanish from Tenochtitlán in a battle the Spanish referred to as La Noche Triste ("Night of Sadness"). While the Spanish regrouped, an epidemic broke out in the Aztec capital. Among its victims was Cuitláhuac. His death ended his reign only eighty days after it started.

Itzcoatl

Itzcoatl, the fourth Aztec tlatoani, reigned from 1427 to 1440. While in power, Itzcoatl oversaw a successful war between the Aztecs and the Tepanecs. As a result, in 1428 Itzcoatl was able to ally Tenochtitlán with two nearby cities, Texcoco and Tlacopan. In this Triple Alliance, the three peoples promised not to battle with each other and to divide the wealth obtained by fighting other groups. Because of the Triple Alliance, the Aztecs emerged as the most powerful people in the Valley of Mexico. In Aztec histories, Itzcoatl was credited with founding the empire.

Juan Diego

Born in 1474, Juan Diego was a poor Aztec farmer living north of Tenochtitlán. After the fall of the Aztec Empire, he converted to Catholicism. In 1531, while walking to a church for religious instruction, Diego had a vision of the Virgin Mary, who spoke to him in Nahuatl, his native language. Known as the Virgin of Guadalupe, Diego's vision has since become an important focus of devotion for Catholics throughout Latin America. The Catholic Church made Juan Diego a saint in 2002.

La Malinche

La Malinche, known as Doña Maria to the Spanish, was from a noble Aztec family. After the death of her father, a local leader, her mother sold La Malinche into slavery. When Hernán Cortés arrived on the Gulf Coast in 1519, area Indians presented La Malinche to the Spanish leader as a peace offering. La Malinche accompanied Cortés's army, serving as a translator throughout their conquest of the Aztec empire. She also became Cortés's mistress and bore him a son named Martín. In Mexico today, she remains a controversial figure. Some consider her a traitor to her people. Others celebrate her as a heroine of early Mexican history.

Motecuhzoma I

Born in 1397, Motecuhzoma I, also known as Motecuh-zoma Ilhuicamina, succeeded Itzcoatl as tlatoani. During his reign (1440 - 1469), Motecuhzoma I concentrated on expanding the Aztec Empire. He took over territory through military conquest, then demanded tribute from the conquered people. (This system would be employed by all the tlatoque who followed him.) Motecuhzoma I was also notable for his large-scale building projects, including enlarging the temple to the god Huitzilopochtli in Tenochtitlán, and for codifying Aztec law.

Motecuhzoma II

The great grandson of Motecuhzoma I, Motecuhzoma II, also known as Motecuhzoma Xocoyotzin, was a priest and a warrior before succeeding his uncle Ahuitzotl as the Aztec tlatoani. Reigning from 1502 to 1520, Motecuh-zoma was well regarded by his people before the arrival of Hernán Cortés and his Spanish army in 1519. As Cortés's men marched toward Tenochtitlán, Motecuhzoma repeat-edly sent ambassadors to meet with the Spanish leader, but otherwise did nothing to impede their invasion. Possi-bly, Motecuhzoma believed Cortés was the embodiment of the Aztec god Quetzalcoatl. After Motecuhzoma wel-comed Cortés into the Aztec capital, Cortés immediately took him captive. Motecuhzoma was murdered in June of 1520, either by the Spanish or by his people.

Tizoc

The brother of and successor to Axayacatl, Tizoc served an undistinquished reign that lasted only five years (1481 - 1486). His only true achievement as tlatoani was expand-ing the Templo Mayor complex. Tizoc, whose name meant "Chalk Leg," was a particularly weak military leader. Sources suggest that he may have been poisoned by peo-ple in his own court.

archaeologist person who studies archaeology

archaeology the study of human-made objects to learn about past ways of life

artifact handmade object, such as a tool or a weapon, that can be studied to learn about a past culture

atole thin soup flavored with chilis or fruit

calmecac school for the children of Aztec nobles

chinampa system of farming in which plots are built up from fertile soil in swampy land

codex (codices, plural) collection of handwritten pages, often containing an ancient text

conquest the act of conquering a foreign territory

elite having high status

empire large territory governed by a powerful ruler

excavation a cavity that is dug up to find buried objects

expedition journey taken by a group of people for a specific purpose

famine severe shortage of food leading to mass hunger

Huitzilopochtli patron god of the Aztecs

macehualtin commoners in Aztec society

Mesoamerica region including present-day Mexico, Guatemala, Belize, and parts of Honduras and El Salvador

metate grinding stone

obsidian sharp volcanic rock used by the Aztecs to make weapons and tools

pipiltin nobles in Aztec society

pochteca Aztec traders who dealt in exotic goods

pulque fermented alcoholic beverage consumed by Aztec nobles during ceremonies

quachtli cotton capes worn by Aztec nobles

tlamacazton young nobles in training to become Aztec priests

tlamatinime wisemen or priests of the Aztec

tlatoani (tlatoque, plural) Aztec emperor

tonalpohualli Aztec calendar in which a year was made up of 260 days

tribute tax paid by the people of the Aztec Empire

whorl weighted disk used to control the speed of a spindle or spinning wheel

Books

Baquedano, Elizabeth. *Aztec, Inca & Maya.* New York: DK Publishing, 2000.

Gruzinski, Serge. *The Aztecs: Rise and Fall of an Empire.* New York: Harry N. Abrams, 1992.

Israel, Fred L., ed. *Ancient Civilizations of the Aztecs and Maya: Chronicles from National Geographic.* Philadelphia: Chelsea House, 1999.

MacDonald, Fiona. *How Would You Survive As an Aztec?* New York: Franklin Watts, 1995.

Morgan, Nina. *Technology in the Time of the Aztecs.* Austin, TX.: Raintree/Steck Vaughn, 1998.

Stein, R. Conrad. *The Aztec Empire.* Tarrytown, NY: Benchmark Books, 1996.

Organizations and Online Sites

Aztecs
http://www.aztecs.org.uk

England's Royal Academy of Arts packs this site with engaging text and illustrations dealing with Aztec art, history, and culture.

Aztecs on EduScapes
http://www.42explorea.com/aztec.htm

The educational site EduScapes offers many links to pages about the Aztecs for students and teachers.

Civilizations in America
http://www.wsu.edu/~dee/CIVAMRCA/AZTECS.HTM

Washington State University provides a wealth of information about the Aztecs and other ancient peoples, including the Toltecs and the Maya.

History of Chocolate
http://www.fieldmuseum.org/Chocolate/history.html

Based on a popular museum exhibit, this site explores the role chocolate played in the culture of several ancient peoples, including the Aztecs.

Mexico City
http://www.mexicocity.com.mx/history1.html

This virtual guide to Mexico City discusses its Aztec past as well as the city's present-day attractions.

The Sport of Life and Death: The Mesoamerican Ballgame
http://www.ballgame.org

Using inventive graphics, this site examines the place of ball games in ancient Mesoamerican cultures.

Templo Mayor Museum
http://archaeology.la.asu.edu/tm/index2.htm

This museum site offers information about the Aztecs obtained through the ongoing excavation of the Templo Mayor in Mexico City.

Teotihuacán: The City of the Gods
http://archaeology.la.asu.edu/teo/INDEX.php

Established by Arizona State University, this heavily illustrated site is devoted to Teotihuacán, the ancient city much admired by the Aztecs.

About the Author

Liz Sonneborn is a writer and editor living in Brooklyn, New York. A graduate of Swarthmore College, she has written more than forty books for children and adults, including *The American West*, *A to Z of American Women in the Performing Arts*, and *The New York Public Library's Amazing Native American History*, winner of a 2000 Parent's Choice Award.